BUILD YOUR SPIRITUAL LIFE

INTIMATE RELATIONSHIP WITH GOD

ISBN: 9798847897679

TABLE OF CONTENTS

INTRODUCTION

You could contemplate at times, whether the lessons and illustrations of the Bible have significance in your life today. You could likewise contemplate whether you have time a superior relationship with yourself, others and with God. This is really the absolute best time for you to consider enabling your spirituality by beginning to carry on with an existence with God generally in your heart and mind. Continuously consider the sort of relationship that you have with Him and with individuals around you.

Never make promises that you can't keep. You can take a glance at your past, and you can forgive yourself. You can decide to become pitchers or hitters. You can likewise break those horrible cycles, and in particular, you can pursue choices to move into a more significant, more profound relationship with God. He will direct you in constantly. Just consistently remember Him, and consistently think about Him in every choice that you make, all the days of your life, and you will experience how he will change your life for good.

CHAPTER 1
MAKE YOUR MIND UP

The vast majority dwell in their past mistakes and failures so much that they become spiritually weak or even death. You need to remember that you are human and no human is above mistake.
Stop dwelling in your past mistakes, you need to focus on what's ahead of you.

Your mistakes don't define you and they do not need to define your future if you choose not to, they can be help to shape your future. It all boils down to you. To further develop your spirituality, only a couple of changes in life can carry massive impacts in your life and can help move you closer to your goal of spiritual growth.

To have more understanding on how to improve your spirituality, I've laid down some points:

As you make your new year resolution each year it's advisable to get your priorities straight. Think about your needs this year.

You should stop smoking, practice more or get in shape. You should wipe out your toxic relationships, or begin fostering a more grounded relationship with your partner, friends or family. Anything you desire, recall that your most prominent need us to create a stronger and intimate relationship with God.

Perhaps of the main thing that you want to recall is to forgive yourself of your past. To love yourself really mean being able to forgive yourself of your previous mistakes, then loving yourself and God should be your priority, you can begin depending on Him for your direction.

At the point when you begin putting your needs on drawing nearer to Him, and when you seek first the kingdom of God and his righteousness, He will constantly direct you. Maybe, it is the best resolution that you ought to make - to strengthen your relationship with God and seek first the kingdom of God.

This is the best time for you to sincerely promise to invest your time on Him and consistently thinking about God in each decision that you make and each day of your life. Spend time daily in praying and getting intimate with God every day, Spend quality time reading the word of God letting his word to guide you, to be a lamp unto your feet and a light unto your path. Besides, you really want to remember that beginning a spiritual resolution isn't all about reading the Holy Bible; it is likewise about thinking of Him in each choice and decision that you make.

Utilize your better judgment and your wisdom in picking. At the point to make a good or a bad decision, consistently think about how your decision will affect your relationship with God.

At the point when you commit mistakes, never permit yourself to feel down, particularly when you stumble. Continuously keep up with the right attitude. You additionally don't need to do things alone. This is the authentic purpose for your community of faith. You will constantly have a source of strength to help one another.

CHAPTER 2
SELF-COMPASSION

At times, individuals are extremely awful and unforgiving to themselves. Imagine you committed an enormous error on a specific task at work, making more work for your colleagues and yourself, or you could incidentally said something dumb on a first date or at an important meeting. What will really be your reaction?

You need to remember that taking care of yourself doesn't have to mean a regular visit to the spa. It simply implies treating yourself the manner in which you treat an old buddy of yours.

Many individuals would respond in such circumstances by rebuking themselves for their mistakes. In such case, you are metaphorically pounding yourself. In a little portion, self-criticism can really be extremely useful on the grounds that it persuades individuals to assume responsibilities of every one of their actions, and it urges them to additionally work on themselves. In any case, to much self-criticism can be debilitating and defeating.

Self-compassion is truly significant. It implies treating one's self with understanding and consideration once you commit a misstep, or go through a perplexing circumstance, simply the manner in which you treat others you care about.

This is very that somehow the same with self-esteem, yet it's the manner in which you are treating yourself and not how you are judging yourself. In this manner, whether you are believing that you are an extraordinary individual or not at any moment in your life, you can have empathy for yourself. For example, you could say that it is fine to commit an error; you will simply put more effort into it next time.

There are various methods towards building compassion, and one of which is having the option to move your point of view. For sure, it is very more straightforward for us to give sympathy to others than it is for us to give it to ourselves. In such case, it very well may be better assuming you begin treating yourself better.

You can imagine that an individual you care about is from your shoes. Ponder the things that you would tell them. You could really say something kinder and better to yourself.

You additionally need to recollect that one of the main requirements for compassion is having the conviction that you, very much like some other individuals, consistently deserves being treated with adoration and empathy. Building compassion can likewise assist you with safeguarding you from those destructive people.

Maybe, one of the essential keys for you to be continually good to yourself is to continuously believe in yourself and have more confidence in your abilities. Try not to be too hard in yourself and figure out how to acknowledgment your accomplishments. Through this, you will witness massive changes in your life.

CHAPTER 3
PRAYER

God has gives us a lot of tools for our survival, yet none can truly contrast with the ability of speaking with Him in prayer. Praying to God is really not simply your most important instruments; it can moreover be your most exceptional asset.

In this world of preliminaries and challenges, it is very difficult for individuals to stay unshakeable. Things are becoming harder, and without a particular source of strength, you will most likely be unable to get by in this life. Since God cherishes every one of His children, He equips us with an important instrument that we can use to strengthen ourselves - PRAYER

Praying to God is one of key ways for you to speak with Him and get intimate with Him. It is a significant means for a day to day discussion with God. The importance of praying to God everyday can't be overestimated. Presently, for you to completely comprehend its worth, you need to take a closer look at essence and how important praying to God everyday is.

Prayer gives individuals the chance to impart all aspects in life with the Heavenly Father. Life's conditions generally change consistently, and what's in store is yet unknown. Truly, things can constantly go from great to more regrettable in an exceptionally brief timeframe. God believes that we should carry their burdens and worries to Him so He can help us, and He want them to draw nearer to Him constantly.

With each blessing that you get in this life, prayer gives you a means to offer your thanks for everything in this life that He gives. Obviously, you should continually express gratefulness to God for all that He gives. You pray to recognize every one of the blessing overflow that you have as a result of Him.

All individuals commit mistakes every day, and they all sin each day, regardless of whether they it willingly or not. You are flawed yet God believes you should admit your sin and ask for forgiveness, and you can accomplish this through prayer. This offers the stage for you to admit your transgressions and repent. Through prayer, you allow yourself an ideal opportunity to release the weight that you carry in your souls.

Prayer is likewise a demonstration of obedience and love. In 1 Thessalonians 5:16-18, you can distinguish the significance of praying consistently. "Rejoice always, pray without ceasing, in everything give thanks; for this is the will of God in Christ Jesus for you.." It is the desire of the Lord for every one of His children to express appreciation and pray to Him. This is a demonstration of dutifulness and love that gives incredible pleasure to God. He loves to see every one of His kids following His rules.

Many people realize that a preeminent being is in charge of things and of their lives, and through prayer, they recognize this reality.

God is incomparable and nothing truly occurs without Him being familiar with it. Daily, you really need to acknowledge Him in your life.

Through prayer, you express your love towards Him.

To accomplish something, prayer is likewise perhaps the best tool that you can use to accomplish your heart's desires. Nonetheless, individuals once in a while feel that God doesn't answer every one of their prayers. You really want to remember that God knows it all, and He understands what you need even before you request it. All He maintains that you should do is to be devoted in Him.

Assuming you have been asking exactly the same thing, and it appears to be that God isn't answering your prayers or not giving what you need, He wants you to learn something. God really answers your prayers in three ways - Yes, No and Wait.

He would reply "Yes" assuming He realizes that it is fitting for you, "No" in the event that it will be if no good you and "Wait" since there is a perfect time for everything. He likewise wants you to put your faith in HIM. You should be patient. He adores every one of His children and He knows precisely the exact thing they need even before they ask it. God realizes what is best as far as we're concerned; you should simply to have faith in Him.

CHAPTER 4
STUDY THE WORD OF GOD

Most times, people feel that things are turning out to be much more terrible and more confounded. They pray everyday except it appears to be that God isn't noting their prayers. In such case, you should evaluate your life. What is lacking? What are the things that you want to change and do?

If you have any desire to enhance your spirituality, praying isn't exactly enough; concentrating on God's lessons through perusing the scriptures is additionally exceptionally significant. Making time consistently to concentrate on God's lessons will bring changes into your life, particularly when you put to practice what you have learnt.

In any case, the issue with many people is that they need time because of their tight schedule. Yet, to work on your life, you can always make time. To assist you with dealing with your time and see a greater amount of His lessons, there are a few significant things you want to remember.

People usually find it hard to find energy and time to read the scriptures, however if you have the zeal to study the word of God, you will create time no matter how busy or tired you are.

You need to commit time to study His word. Set aside a specific time to study His word and always keep to that time. If you are serious about understanding the sacred writings and developing your insight about God's promise, then, at that point, you additionally must be intense about concentrating on it.

God believes that His children should concentrate on His words, so He is assisting us with concentrating on the entirety of His words; all we want to do is to go to Him and consistently ask Him in prayer. Remember that the Word of God and Prayer generally remain inseparable. These are both significant while contemplating.

At the point when you begin to study His words, you want to have a reason. What is it that you need to learn? What principle could you need to learn more? Continuously pray for assist in picking a reason and you see how meaningful your scripture study will be.

You might take notes as you study the scriptures. This can help you more to completely comprehend the importance of the things you have found. Studying on his teachings additionally includes great effort and faith, so you really want to grasp these things, and you will perceive the way your life will change.

CHAPTER 5 MEDITATE

If you are looking for fulfilment in your life, vibrant health, calmness and joy, you can acquire these things through the power of meditation.

This gives endless advantages to your spirit, brain and body. Making time to meditate brings a many more advantages beside things like this, and they are wished to be uncovered through digging further into this part.

Meditation is a really important instrument that assists people with cultivating actual wellbeing, combat stress, become more peaceful, feel more joyful, can assist them with sleeping better and it can assist you with working on your life.

Be that as it may, on a more profound sense, meditation is a significant entryway into the unknown. This can assist you with getting a feeling of the entire mystery of your personalities and who you truly are.

At the point when you create time to meditate, you are likewise helping yourself towards accomplishing a ultimate objective of meditation, which is edification. It is the acknowledgment of your mind's true nature. Through drawing further into your consciousness and directing your mind, you can find reality, and by developing such practice, you can begin developing a positive way to deal with your lives.

Meditation means quite a lot to your mind. Over the course of the day, your mind is loaded up with different thoughts. At the point when you begin making time to meditate, you are concentrating at your soul's seat, and afterward you start to quite your mind.

By meditation regularly, you are fostering a sustainable concentration. Such expansion in concentration got together with diminished pressure and stress, further developed relationship and reestablished energy can assist you with acquiring success in your activities.

Meditation is a spiritual encounter that engages your spirit, and empowers you to ascend into different dimensions of higher consciousness . By centering your attention inside, you are really ready to encounter those inward realms and you relationship with God, consequently fulfilling the genuine reason for your existence.

What is inside every one of us is really a heavenly spirit. The method involved with getting to such internal spirit, insight and knowledge is known as meditation. You can engage your spirituality by creating time to meditate.

CHAPTER 6
YOUR INNER VOICE

You can lay out extraordinary insight by consistently spending time in thankful fellowship and figuring out how to pay attention to your inward voice.

There is no any better approach to laying out a satisfying life than through knowing the art of being in tune with your inspired self - your internal voice. Such voice fills in as your aide in this complicated life. Through figuring out how to stand by listening to it, you will know the extraordinary changes that it can bring into your life.

Each individual has an inward voice; you only simply need to listen and pay attention to is so it can lead you. If you keep on standing by, listening to it, then you can begin to live a true and fulfilled life. To assist you with remaining on top of your inner voice, there are a few significant things you really want to remember;

You have an inward voice, it's not a critical parent, an addictive personality or a compulsive spender inside your head. It comes from the piece of who you are that can help you in real life expressions. It doesn't yell; it really talks and speaks with you from a point of silence inside you.

Since it's an calm voice, you must be still and quiet to be able to hear it. If your mind is loaded up with worry, longing, resentment, stress, grief or fear, you will never hear this voice.

It really takes practice to hear this voice. Hearing your deepest desires is difficult.

This is similar to what's meant by trusting or listening to your inner voice. Figure out how to perceive your inner voice and you can do this by being in a condition of calmness and quietness. You want to clear your thoughts of all those pointless things that act as boundary to hearing it.

One of the best mysteries of remaining in tune with your inner voice and understanding its messages is really having a heart that is loaded up with love and appreciation. Open your heart, open it with great gratitude, and you will see that your internal voice will try and become stronger and more clear. What it

needs will be brought into your mind easily

CHAPTER 7
YOUR MINDSET

Your perspective has significant impacts in your life today and to the days to come. If you center your mindset into the positive things in your life, you will likewise have a more joyful life than you might at any point consider.

Altering your perspective about being positive can likewise completely changes you. This will empower you to improve your current situation. It will give you hope of a better tomorrow. Shifting your mindset into being optimistic will empower you to see a more brighter side of life regardless of how hard or complicated life might be.

If you keep on having a positive mindset, you can make a more certain life. Nonetheless, with the difficult circumstances that people are encountering, it turns out to be very difficult for them to think of the positive side of this life; however every one of us need to imagine that there are ways of working on your life, and one of which is to figure out how to be positive and impact our perspective.

With the difficulties and challenges that many people face in life, it is very hard not to be pessimistic thoughts in this life. It is difficult to shift your mind into optimistic thoughts, when things are getting difficult around you. In any case, you need to understand that if you need to end your sufferings, you want to take charge and it begins with the manner in which you reason about life.

There are numerous positive activities that you can really do to build your positive mental attitude, and it initially starts with your thought process. If you generally believe that "you can't", then, at that point, you are attempting to persuade that really you can't. Think positive and use expressions of assertions towards yourself.

You want to push out every one of the gloomy feelings that you have in you. Try not to allow those gloomy feelings like doubt, anxiety, fear, and the likes to overpower you. Continuously center around the positive side of life. You want to remember what is happening, there is continuously something better you can get. Figure out how to perceive those things. Continuously contemplate the positive things in life.

Something else that you can do is to utilize words that induce strength, power and achievement. Fill your mind with words that will cheer you up more. Having an impact on your mindset about being positive can assist you with encountering a seriously satisfying and promising life you generally care about. Be positive and you will likewise draw in great things in your life.

CHAPTER 8
BE GRATEFUL

At the point when you figure out how to develop an appreciative mindset, it will turn out to be almost impossible for you to be empty, sad or frustrated, The entire universe is energy and energy is a never-ending power. In this manner, what you need comes from energy.

To guarantee that you will get the positive things in life, you likewise need to have a thankful mindset.

Life is loaded with uncertainty, and when things don't turn out well for you, it turns out to be more difficult to dwell on the positive side of life. Be that as it may, if you need to work on your life, and guarantee a positive future in front of you, you want to change now. Get a thankful perspective and continually develop it.

When you're really thankful for an occasion, a situation, someone or something, you are sending an extraordinary state of energy into the universe and afterward, the universe will answer it. If you keep on growing a thankful mindset and take a look at the brighter side of life, the universe will likewise get positively transform you.

To build your thankful mindset, you want to shift your concentration from those things that you don't have, or you lack towards those that you have in abundance. Be thankful about life and to every small blessings that you received. Figure out how to perceive the best things that are going on in your life as opposed to concentrating on the opposite.

At the point when you build a thankful mindset, you will get positive changes in your life. You will likewise feel that regardless of how hard life can be or the way in which harder your problems are, you actually carry on with a more joyful life. Remember that your happiness doesn't rely upon others; it generally relies upon you. Your opinion on life today will manifest from now on. Continuously be appreciative for what you have, and center around the great things life offers you.

CHAPTER 9
AFFIRMATION

What you ceaselessly think and talk about life will manifest in the sort of life that you have. If you accept and feel that you can follow through with something, then you can, so you should be cautious with your thoughts.

Giving yourself motivational affirmation can get you moving on regardless of how difficult your circumstances might be. The words of motivational affirmation are more powerful than you think. Your belief system and your attitude that can develop your life and will make your become successful.

If you have any desire to remain on the course and keep on carrying on with the type of life that you need, you want to utilize the power of affirmation. All people have ability to alter their direction of life, and utilizing affirmation, you can bring significant changes into your lives.

You can accomplish your desires and acquire what your heart wants provided that you accept that you can do as such. Affirmation are really declaration you say to yourself or you say so anyone might hear. You are affirming to yourself that anything you want will happen.

Affirmation work since anything you repeat to yourself will significantly impact your thoughts, and whatever you center your mind around, you will draw in, and getting what your heart wants.

While utilizing affirmation, you need to guarantee that you affirmation are positive words. Utilize such statement to mirror the things you need to occur or objectives you need to accomplish.

Keep in mind that your life is actually outer manifestations of your inner beliefs and thoughts. Affirmation are simple and straightforward yet extremely strong. A great deal of businesspeople have involved them to successfully maintain their business. Numerous specialists have likewise utilized them to turn out to be more imaginative and use it to come up with great ideas. You also can get benefit from its power in each aspect of your life.

Focused affirmation act as ideal ways for you to begin your day to day activities and live the kind of life you want, At the point when you experience torment, feel stress, strain or simply any sort of anxiety, insistences can constantly encourage you. The ability to control your life is inside you. You are answerable for the sort of life you have.

Affirmation are enormously strong, and they have the ability to deeply influence your life and possibly to lay out a life of harmony and joy.

Remember that only your thoughts can keep you from reaching your goals and such thoughts can be adjusted. This is a significant process that will change the manner in which you view life, and also the overall quality of life.

CHAPTER 10
SPIRITUAL RESOLUTION

Spiritual resolutions completely changes your life positively. You may not realize it but by laying out spiritual resolutions, you are working on your life and building your spirituality.

In this complex and mischievous world, thinking about your spirituality is very hard. More often than not, individuals are excessively occupied with their lives and they fail to remember the most important part of their life. This is presently the absolute best time for them to have some time off, stop, and search their lives.

Building your spirituality through spiritual resolutions can assist you with giving harmony and joy to your life.

While making a rundown of resolutions, many individuals generally fail to remember one significant perspective – their spirituality. You want to remember that spiritual resolution can turn into a significant resource in assisting you with fulfilling your objectives, or adapt to a ton of things inside your life you needs to be changed.

This is the best time for you to commit to important spiritual responsibilities that can assist you with working on your life, relationship with your family, companions, accomplice, and your relationship with God. At the point when you start to make spiritual resolutions, you can encounter a more joyful life.

At the point when you start making a spiritual resolution, you likewise start to encounter an life of peace and harmony and consistent joy. You can see the value in the magnificence of life and you will generally consistently check out at the more splendid side of everything.

Your spiritual resolution will assist you with trusting that there will be better days ahead, and this will assist you with continuously drawing closer with faith in God. Spend time and energy figuring out God's lessons and never stop praying to God until your prayers are answered. Make a life of faith and love.

Life has it's 'ups' and 'downs', but with a spiritual resolution, you can live a more meaningful and delighted life. Move ahead in Faith.

www.ingramcontent.com/pod-product-compliance
Lightning Source LLC
LaVergne TN
LVHW020524160826
845677LV00015B/3878